DATING VS. COURTSHIP

And Everything In Between

DATING VS. COURTSHIP
AND EVERYTHING IN BETWEEN
By Sean L. Brereton

Copyright © 2016

All Rights Reserved. No part of this book may be reproduced or utilized in any form or by any means, electronic or mechanical, including photocopying, recording, or by any information storage and retrieval system, without permission in writing from the publisher.

Unless otherwise referenced, Scripture quotations are taken from the King James Version.

For more information, visit the author's website:

seanlbrereton.com

ISBN-13:978-1540849472
ISBN-10:1540849473

Dedication

When someone gives you a gift, say, "Thank you" and show your gratitude in the manner in which you treat that gift. God is ever so gracious to give us the gift of love. The Bible says you can have faith to move mountains, but if you don't have love, you don't have anything (1 Corinthians 13:2). Let us treat that gift with care, as we love one another, show respect for one another, outdo one another in honor, and treat one another with the utmost love and respect. With that said, this book is dedicated to you as a token of my love. God gave me a gift. Thank you for allowing me to share it with you.

I dedicate this book to the reader, for opening pages of my heart and allowing my voice to be heard.

CONTENTS

Dedication v

Intro ix

Chapter 1 This Thing Called Dating 1

    When Dating is Problematic... 2

    Guard your Heart 3

Chapter 2 What is Courtship? 9

    Steps in Courtship 11

    Counsel... 15

    Courtship.. 15

    The Don'ts of Courtship.. 17

    Protect Your Courtship 19

Chapter 3 Recovering from a Break Up 23

    Poem: Wintered Memories.. 25

    Poem: Hopeless Promises 27

    What Every Woman Needs to know About Men 27

    The Most Beautiful Arrangement of Broken II 28

    Redefinition of a Man.. 29

    Poem: Love Me Back... 30

    Poem: Deadly Alive.. 30

Chapter 4 Recovering from Abuse 35
I Know How to Handle Him 36
Poem: Gone for Good 38
Poem: I Prayed for You 39
Pray For Healing 41
God is a Healer 42
A Dying Relationship 44
Poem: Holding On 44
Poem: Too Comfortable 46
Poem: Clock Games and Brick Doors 46

Chapter 5 Dating vs. Courtship 51
Pinpointing the Counterfeit 52
Dating vs. God's Commandments 54
God is Not the Author of Situationships 59
The Straight and Narrow Way 60
Dating vs. Courtship Quiz 62

Chapter 6 Help from the Experts 67
The Fatal Attraction 69
The XY Theory 72
1__1=1 75
Self-Identity 76
Unequally-Yoked 82
Culture and Religion 83

Chapter 7 Help from God 85

    God's Timing 85

        Poem: You Deserve More 85

    Timing Is Everything 86

    The Beauty in Single 87

        Poem: Nightly Visitors 90

    God's Timing Is Perfect 91

    Finding the Right One 94

        Poem: It's You 94

    A Happy Ending 97

        Poem: Grace 98

Thank You 101

More from the Author 103

Contact Me 107

Bibliography 109

Intro

Jonathan and Brittney were friends for more than ten years. For most of the time they've known each other their interactions were strictly platonic; though somewhere along the course of friendship, feelings began to bud. Brittney reached out to me excited and anxious. She asked a ton of questions. *Do you think it would work? I really like him, but I don't know if he feels the same! Can he be the one?* These were all great questions to ask; but before I could even begin to answer, I myself had questions. Brittney recently decided she would no longer date outside of her denomination anymore and was very open to dating Jonathan because he, like her, was a Seventh-day Adventist Christian. They had also begun a 40-day devotional together, which required them to speak and pray together often—I told her this was a horrible idea. Anyway, I don't want to belabor the point of this story. Jonathan and Brittney, both huge fans of poetry, planned the perfect *date*—a poetry concert. It wasn't before long Brittney in distress contacted me with bad news. "Him and I shouldn't be happening... He is courting someone!" I immediately responded with an apology to hear the news and began to slowly unpack what I had heard. *Aren't they really good friends (of ten years)? How didn't she know this? Courting? I wonder if he understood what courting really was. If he cannot practice safe boundaries with a female friend, how can he do so with whomever he was courting?* Unfortunately, some Christians unknowingly Christianize dating and call it courtship without realizing the subtle and not so subtle dangers.

Brittney's perfect date didn't end well. If you describe the perfect date, where would it be? Who would it be with? What would you do? Recently, while helping a friend move, I met a young lady that said she was sick of relationships. I asked her why so? The first thing she said before going any deeper was, "Love is depressing..." I'm sure she is not the only person to feel this way. Some of us may deny it because the feeling of being in love is so alluring! But many people are burnt and so full of resentment for the opposite sex. What if I told you that ninety percent of romantic relationships are designed to fail? Now that I have your attention, what if I can help you understand why? Now, I am no expert, but I have learned so much through my failures and the experiences of others, and I am always eager to share what I know. I certainly believe that love can work and aspire to help you with your relationships. Every relationship doesn't have to end or even worse, end in heartbreak. Hopefully, throughout the course of this book, you may find and choose a better path for your love life.

My story begins with Patrice. No, you do not know her. It is a fictitious name for her protection. Anyway, some of the worst arguments I've ever had with anyone in my life were with her. She was one of the most contentious ex-girlfriends of mine. I can confidently admit this was my worst relationship of all time—I despised her! She had a habit of being untruthful, especially when she would mention the details of the boys in her life that she classified as friends. There was one boy in particular whom I couldn't stand; well, it wasn't really him, it was because of my ex and her dishonesty in regards to her interactions with him. It also didn't help my insecurities that he was like the best looking boy in her high school. For a while he was her good "friend" until I found out that they had been intimate in the past. I made it clear that I was not comfortable with the two of them remaining friends. Consequently, I lost whatever trust I had in her.

Today, I have nothing against Patrice. I made a ton of mistakes that propelled her to receive the nomination for the worst relationship. Also, in retrospect, I was a hypocrite. During my yearlong relationship with her (consisting of arguments, fights, breakups and makeups), I wasn't always truthful or honest with my mother and this only served to fuel many arguments between her and me. It's interesting how when things are shaky between you and your partner, you tend to take your anger out on your immediate family. I was very critical of my ex for her bad habits, but I was equally guilty if not worst!

Many years later after learning about courtship there are scores of things I learned from this experience, which I will be sharing as we move along in the course of the book. Firstly, my ex and I were incompatible. We didn't really have much in common except for our ethnicity (we didn't even share the same denomination.) Secondly, I shouldn't have been dating at that time. I was too young. I was a freshman in College and still getting to know myself. I didn't know what my life purpose was. Thirdly, we crossed emotional boundaries which made things gruesomely complicated (as we tried to force-fit a wrong match) and entirely unbearable when we eventually separated.

Ironically, though the nature of our relationship was disastrous, we professed to love one another. We even spoke about marriage at one point even though, whether spiritually or emotionally, I was in no position to be married. Being together for a little more than a year became a license to deem our dysfunctional and volatile situation tolerable. Eventually, unable to handle the stress, I ended the relationship. If I didn't call things off with her and we continued dating, we could've ended up being married—God forbid. Premature and incompatible marriages happen often leaving two people miserable and dangerously unhappy—far from God's goal in marriage.

Many people get married prematurely because of infatuation or move forward into marriage because they were able to endure each other for X amount of years despite a high level of discord. The quality of your relationship during your dating or courtship experience doesn't magically beautify once you are married. If you and your partner spend most of your time quarrelling and fighting, these undesired experiences will also be very present in your marriage. God does not want this for you. For us all, He wants the very best.

So did you figure out who you would want to share that perfect date with yet? Well, let me ask you this, would you like to court this person or date him or her? You may not understand the difference between both, so let's explore beginning with the more recognizable term, dating.

Chapter 1
This Thing Called Dating

Dating, according to the Oxford Dictionary of English, is to "go out with (someone in whom one is romantically or sexually interested)." Does this definition suggest a long-term interest, a mere sexual gratification, or just a casual experience to pass the time? Maybe it depends on the agreement made between the two individuals concerned? But don't we sometimes mask our intentions? Of course! Manipulation and deceit are two of the main issues with the dating scene. Charm in his best suit is still nothing but a façade, and decency is usually short-lived—love too following suit.

I am well aware that dating may mean different things for different people. Also, there are two other variations for the definition of dating we can consider. The first, being in a committed or romantic relationship with one person. We aren't naive enough to assume that every person in a romantic relationship is committed. Hence, one of the reasons you may be reading this. The second, going out with different candidates during the same time period to determine who is a suitable mate. Regardless of the definition, the behaviors usually have a propensity to be the same.

When Dating is Problematic

One thing that I learned from my former relationship is that the manner in which a man treats his mother may be reflective of the manner in which he is likely to treat his wife. Every time I argued with my ex-girlfriend who I spoke of earlier, I was making preparations to be a bickering husband. One of the issues with dating is, sometimes, we see the red flags and know someone is not good for us but we allow our feelings to keep us onboard.

> *"Whatever happens, happens."*
>
> *"I'll just go with the flow."*
>
> *"We'll see where things end up"*

One of the most dangerous things you can do is give your love to someone unworthy.

We would rather wait until the next exit, because it's convenient—and so comfortable, while temptation continues to impair our judgment. Then, we feel as if we might as well stay for the full ride and see where the relationship goes. Get out as soon as you notice that someone is leading you somewhere you're not supposed to be. Get out before you get comfortable. My physical attraction to Patrice made me fall in to something that was not easy to get out of. The emotional attraction made it difficult to sever the physical attachment.

How was my dating experience with Patrice different from God's way of experiencing love?

_____
_____
_____
_____
_____

> *Your relationship should be drawing you closer to Christ, not closer to sin.*

True love is a plant that needs culture. Let the woman who desires a peaceful, happy union, who would escape future misery and sorrow, inquire before she yields her affections; has my lover a mother? What is the stamp of her character? Does he recognize his obligations to her? Is he mindful of her wishes and happiness? If he does not respect and honor his mother, will he manifest respect and love, kindness and attention, toward his wife? When the novelty of marriage is over, will he love me still? Will he be patient with my mistakes, or will he be critical, overbearing, and dictatorial? True affection will overlook many mistakes; love will not discern them. The youth trust altogether too much to impulse.[1]

Guard your Heart

We should be more selective in who we allow ourselves to share intimacy with. Dating has a tendency to cloud wise judgment. Maybe if dating resembled the employment

---

[1] Ellen G. White, *The Review and Herald*.

process, there would be far fewer fragments of broken hearts stamped all over the place.

How would the dating scene look if getting into a relationship was like applying for a job? Well, I have got the answer; dating would be like an interview, and our love lives would be a resume. Our exes would be our past employers and fall under relationship experience. It would be a red flag if someone had too many relationships in a short amount of time. If someone was ever fired or dumped, our potential pursuer could inquire about the terms for separation. There would also be a place for references (three professionals and a friend who could verify that you are eligible to date). Sounds funny right when you think about it but that's the truth.

Now, if you don't mind, here's your interview:

1. What is your definition of dating?

_____
_____
_____
_____
_____
_____

2. After reconsidering the practices typical in dating, what are some things you do not want in your relationship?

_____
_____
_____
_____
_____
_____

3. If you are single, after knowing what you now know and while reflecting on your past mistakes, can you be more selective with whom you decide to be in a relationship with? What are some things you do not want in a partner?

___

You should be prayerful and realistic while considering a life partner. Remember we are all flawed, and no one is perfect.

4. What are some things you do want in a partner?

___

5. Prayerfully re-establish your standards. What are some things you are not willing to compromise or negotiate on?

> **Save the mileage on your heart for the person you are supposed to be going places with. Not everyone deserves to be in a relationship with you.**

Protect your mind and heart from unnecessary experiences that distort your perception of love and happiness. Be selective. Be very selective.

"Keep thy heart with all diligence; for out of it are the issues of life."–Proverbs 4:23

Someone may ask, "Why be so selective?" And those in the church may add, "Especially when there isn't the best group or pool to choose from". I personally believe that it's better to be single than to be mismatched. Mismatched couples are one of the main products of dating. Grief and unhappiness follows suit. If you're unfamiliar with that archaic term **courtship**, let's take a look and see what the *hype* is about.

Chapter 2
What is Courtship?

Google.com offers two definitions for courtship that I want to observe: 1. A period during which a couple develop a romantic relationship, especially with a view to marriage. 2. Behavior designed to persuade someone to marry or develop a romantic relationship with one.

I listed both to see if you can see the distinction between the two. If I had to choose between the two, I would vouch for the first definition. The persuading of someone to marry you may seem innocent, but it is precarious. We are warned of the dangers of these practices in a book, *The Adventist Home*, "Courtship as carried on in this age is a scheme of deception and hypocrisy, with which the enemy of souls has far more to do than the Lord. Good common sense is needed here if anywhere; but the fact is, it has little to do in the matter." There is an element of convincing or persuasion while pursuing, but it should never be your goal to persuade someone into romance or marriage. Your first goal is to seek God's will. Often, under the influence of passion and infatuation, persuasion turns into trickery, dishonesty, deceit and hypocrisy.

This is a more accurate and safe definition of courtship that I've adapted from others: two people considering together whether it's God's will for marriage to be in their future. Simple right? I'd think so. God is a simple God; we are the complex ones. But that is not it. This chapter isn't over just yet. More than that, courtship follows a very particular program. Though different people may carry out their courtships in ways that suit their understanding of it, the outcome should be the same. Courtship, unlike dating, is designed for two reasons: to glorify God and to protect you and your romantic partner.

Though I go into more detail on the proper courtship process in my book, A *Foretaste of Heaven*, I'll sum up some important points so we are on the same page.

The first thing to note about courtship is that it should only happen after God gives your confirmation. The wise man said, "There are many devices in a man's heart; nevertheless, the counsel of the LORD, that shall stand" (Proverbs 19:21). Imagine working for years; sweat, blood, tears go into a relationship, and right before you anxiously prepare to pop the question, the whole thing disintegrates right before your hopeful eyes. In Psalm 127:1, we read, "A Song of degrees for Solomon. Except the LORD build the house, they labour in vain that build it: except the LORD keep the city, the watchman waketh but in vain." Do you want to labor in vain or do you want God to direct your path?

Before we begin our discussion on the steps in courtship, let's see what our motives are regarding the opposite sex.

1. Why do you want companionship? Is it because you are lonely? Or is it for self-gratification? Are you honestly content with being single? Have you gotten over your previous relationship? Do you (still) check out your ex partner's social media page?

The best blessings of marriage are reserved for those who desire love in order to better please and serve God. "Proving what is acceptable unto the Lord." Ephesians 5:10.

Before thinking to be romantically involved, shouldn't we know what we want out of it?

List some of your reasons for desiring a romantic relationship.

1. _____

2. _____

3. _____

4. _____

5. _____

6. _____

7. _____

Steps in Courtship

Within courtship, you will not waste your and someone else's time unless you are certain that God is leading you into marriage. The answer to whether marriage is in His will or when comes in due time. But it will only happen after you have a relationship with God. Then sincere prayer, contemplation and Bible study will eventually reveal to you God's plan. Next, after God gives His direction, you have to question if the timing is to your advantage.

This right time is whether you, primarily, are ready. Are you ready spiritually, academically, mentally, emotionally and financially? If you are and you seek God's direction for who would be a potential match, this person must also be ready on all points mentioned. Again, the first thing to consider before the question of who is a suitable companion is asked is if you are ready. After you narrow down on a candidate, then all the above points should also be considered. Let's briefly address each category.

1. **Spiritually ready.** To be ready spiritually means both persons are surrendered God-fearing Christians—both baptized members of the same denomination. I'll touch on the reason why this is important later; but for now, whenever two persons do not share the same religious beliefs, it causes stress on the relationship. Your partner will eventually feel lonely and as if something in your relationship is missing. Sharing a common religious ground allows couples to understand one another better and creates a better environment for lovely simultaneous growth.

2. **Academically ready.** If courtship happens while any of the two persons are in school, romance causes a strain on studies. Either your relationship or school grades or both will suffer. The timing for courtship is also best after both parties know what their life

work is. If you're still in school, it is most likely because you haven't started your life work yet.
3. **Mentally ready.** Mental preparedness encompasses maturity. Do I need to stress this? Though age is not always a marker of maturity, the right age tends to be at adulthood— after the brain is fully developed. One of the unfortunate reasons why couples split is because of a lack of maturity on someone's part. Poor judgment when making decisions, irresponsibility, inefficient time and money managing skills, indolence, selfishness, ineffectiveness and more are all underlying issues when the question of mental preparedness is pondered.
4. **Emotionally ready.** When considering if one is ready emotionally, you have to consider their confidence, level of trust for the opposite sex, whether one is secure with oneself and content. Does this person have peace and is he or she comfortable with being single? Is he or she still emotionally attached to an ex? Are they still mad at or hurt by their ex? These are some questions to think about when the emotional estate is considered.

I think this is a wise question we should all ask ourselves: What can I bring to the table? In other words, what qualities do you possess that would make your next relationship an edifying and worthwhile experience for you and your potential suitor? Will your influence draw your potential partner closer to Christ? What are some things you need to do and learn to better enhance your courtship experience? What do you need to change about yourself before thinking you are ready for courtship?

1. _____

2. _____

3. _____

4. _____

5. _____

6. _____

7. _____

8. _____

9. _____

10. _____

11. _____

12. _____

13. _____

14. _____

15. _____

Counsel

After presenting your case before God in prayer and meditating on the Scriptures, counsel with your older and experienced Bible-believing Christians regarding your decision; it will be helpful if your counselors know both candidates personally. Many questions must be presented. Characters and personalities must be considered for compatibility. After you gain insight from these experienced individuals, more prayer and time with God is needed so He may continue to lead and make impressions on your heart.

If you feel God is leading you to move forward with your decision, by impressions on the heart and by God speaking through others, then counseling with your parents and your potential courting partner's parents is the next step. Gaining the parents' support, blessings and approval is necessary. You, if you are the man, are asking your lady friend's parents for permission to court her. Much prayer and reflection is needed throughout this whole process. Fasting is also advised. While in the stage of courtship, boundaries, goals and expectations need to be discussed and set.

As mentioned, I only provided a nut-shelled version of true courtship here. For a more detailed description, please read *A Foretaste of Heaven*.

Courtship

After a successful courtship where you and your partner learned as much about each other's characters as possible, if you both are convinced that marriage is a part of God's will, the many questions of how your marriage would look and work should be asked. You and your partner should develop a marriage plan, something like a business plan and consider how you two would work together in ministry. The last two stages are engagement and the final, marriage.

That's a lot, right? Well before you toss this book aside, please understand why these steps are so tedious and crucial. Your heart, time and future are undeniably important. In the carefree environment of dating, where in more cases the only prerequisite is attraction, you are way more vulnerable to getting hurt and/or matched with the wrong person. Remember the ex that was mentioned earlier? Physical attraction was our only prerequisite and that's the recipe for disaster.

Think about it, if you are not willing to work hard through the steps to preserve your emotional health and secure happiness before marriage, why would you want to work to keep your marriage? Adhering to principles and boundaries also will help to develop your characters and put you in a better position to trust and grow in God.

Also, because the devil hates God, he will use all in his darkly power to take revenge on God. He accomplishes this in hurting God's children. He is aware that whenever we are hurt, God empathizes. He is well aware also that through romantic relationships, he can cause the most havoc and gloom.

Courtship, as rigid as it may appear, also has a higher success rate. Now before you think to challenge this statement, success doesn't always mean the courtship will end in marriage. But the notion of success always takes emotional and spiritual safety into consideration. If two people court and follow these steps faithfully and the courtship doesn't work out, they have the liberty of separating without hatred, animosity or heartbreak because of the other person. Conversely while dating, in some cases after a tragic breakup, some will even hate God. And Satan is well pleased. Do you see how Satan attempts to ensnare us now through dating or improper courtship?

One of the blessings of courtship is being able to walk away, accepting and respecting that it was not God's will, while still maintaining your dignity and your love and respect for your ex-partner and for God. Do you want headache and heartache or holiness and happiness, or do you want your marriage to be a foretaste of heaven? A failed marriage, a child out of wedlock, the contraction of AIDS or another STD, a broken heart or home are all possible and unfortunate cases that are more likely to occur in the dating scenario.

The Don'ts of Courtship

1. Avoid desperation. After being single for quite some time, I remember meeting this girl. When I first saw her, I was blown away. My initial response to myself was, "Wow, who's that?" So after seeing her once, twice, and then three times, making my smile obvious whenever we would make eye contact, I decided to engage in a friendly dialog. After getting to know her for a couple of days, she openly expressed that she loved me and that God had sent me into her life. I've never heard anything more beautiful sound so unattractive—presumption at its finest. I mean, it sounded desperate. Like a dog can sense when someone may have wrong intentions, we as people can

usually sense when someone reeks of desperation. Most times, men like a catch. They do not respect what comes too easily. When you're desperate, and it shows, you give yourself away. While speaking of desperation, consider what makes someone act desperate? Perhaps it may be emotional ties that are lacking in a home environment with family. Or a brokenness and desire to feel loved. Ask yourself and prayerfully consider, why is he, she or am I so desperate to pursue this person? If you're willing to court anyone, why would he feel special? When you seem very desperate and are still single, would a man be interested in courting you? When you are desperate you exude a strong lack of confidence and a lack of self-respect.

2. Don't be presumptuous. It is dangerous to assume that every godly man with a nice smile who walks into your life is the man God sent for you. Don't let yourself get pumped up with hope too soon. Give yourself the opportunity to discover if you even like the man. You may find yourself flirting with someone God might have allowed into your life for a lesson or simply as encouragement.

3. Don't be aggressive. When you are frantic for love, you tend to come on too strong. Now, this goes to the ladies: Don't give him too much of your time or attention too soon. Your time is something vitally important, and not everyone should feel as if they

deserve it. Value your time, and set boundaries for yourself. Don't give away all your cards too soon. Any man, if he is a gentleman, will be patient and willing to earn your attention, your trust, and eventually, your love.

> *My love is nothing to treat casually. It is not something I give to just anyone. So if I give it to you, I'm telling you it is important to me. If I do, you are important to me. So treat my love as if it is important to you.*

Protect Your Courtship

Protect what you have, but not by being manipulative, controlling, and overprotective. Guard what's yours by loving and treating that person in the manner in which they deserve to be treated.

You don't have to be manipulative; controlling, and overprotective to safeguard what's already yours. When you display these traits, you reveal your insecurity and your lack of confidence. Show your protection for your partner by respecting him or her. Also, always put this person second to God.

You've seen him turn still the life of your rapids and walk on them casually as if nothing happened. Then without warning, the wisdom of his lips would caress your interest, and he would turn those same waters into wine. But two of the best things you can ever do for him are to shield him from you and yourself from him. You shouldn't have any other gods before God.

I'm sure she's beautiful, and I'm sure she is all you've ever dreamed of. I'm also sure your heart beats only for the circulation of her thoughts through your mind. But often, we taint our blessings and allow our relationships to corrupt us. God blesses us, and we turn around and thank Him by replacing God in our lives with the blessing.

I will dissect each commandment that relates to courtship later, but the first commandment says, *"Thou shalt have no other gods before me"* (Exodus 20:3). I'm sure she's the reason flowers bloom in the summer. I know you've never loved anyone like her before. Rightly defend your courtship and your future marriage, but never place anyone before God—not your friends, not your family, not your mother, and not even your courting partner.

Maybe this is one of the many reasons you're still single. Sometimes, because of our idolatrous nature, God would rather save you from harm by keeping you single.

> *I did not hold back. I made myself blindly vulnerable, and it was the biggest risk I ever took, but it was worth it. You are the most beautiful thing I will ever know.*

Another important aspect of protecting your courtship is forgiveness. When you walk in love with someone, it's a leap of faith. You never know where it will take you, or if you will walk out alone. Still something in you compels you to be bold and vulnerable because you know what you deserve. You just have to be hopeful, prayerful, and love like it's your first and last time.

You may be tired of being hurt and seeking for the perfect relationship, but every relationship is the perfect opportunity to get hurt. So when walking into one, make sure if you're willing to love, you're also willing to forgive. Learn from your mistakes, but don't use the mistakes that your previous lover made against your new significant other. Also, never be more willing to receive than you're willing to give, and never ask for what you're not willing to give.

If you prayed for your partner before he entered your life, and you are certain he or she is the one God has sent to you, then forgive him or her at all costs.

People shouldn't pursue romantic relationships because they think the other person is perfect. They desire romance because the person is willing, honest, and trying...

> *If you trust me, you wouldn't be wondering what I was doing every five minutes. If I love you, I wouldn't leave room for doubt. We can both learn to trust each other, while we grow in love. If you're open, you can see I am worth it. If I'm wise, I won't give you reasons to feel like I can't be trusted.*

Set some rules for your relationship, and make some expectations. Your courting partner is not perfect and was not when you met him. He or she will mess up. However, communicate that honesty is critically important to you. If you discover something that could jeopardize your trust in your partner, then make it clear that this behavior threatens your relationship. Now, I'm not condoning separation in terms of dissolving a courtship, but emphasizing the importance for honesty and transparency in your relationship. If your partner is willing and honest enough to address something he or she may have done to disrespect your relationship or something he or she may have been hiding, I support forgiveness and looking past the offense. If he or she isn't honest, I support the termination of this relationship. You cannot love what you cannot trust.

All of the steps in courtship, most of which are not present in dating, are set in place for you and your courting partner's spiritual, emotional, and physical protection. I don't know about you, but my heart is not a toy. Now I'm hoping you have a broader understanding of God's love and why courtship is advised. But someone may still be confused, upset or depressed, suffering from the aftereffects of dating. I've been there too and I got over it, so can you.

Chapter 3
Recovering from a Break Up

For whatever reason, I underwent an unexpected change of heart and took a great amount of time to really love and appreciate the last ex-girlfriend I had dated. After several fights and one last breakup, it seemed to me that we had rekindled our flame after trying to settle our differences; but unfortunately, the relationship was already ruined beyond repair. My ex-girlfriend and I had taken a vow that we would love each other forever. So imagine my shock and astonishment when our relationship eventually unraveled and fell apart. It was even more baffling when she left me. A love that is not repairable is one that is not rooted in the foundation of Christ. Christ's love for us is repairable; it "holds no record of wrong." He always looks past our faults and is still willing to love us. My perception of love at the time was also the world's definition of love, or what we know to be lust. It was not God's definition.

While we were in love, at times I was kind and patient, I was giving and other things—I was able to practice a few characteristics of love that are found in 1 Corinthians 13, but not all of them. This was also true for my ex-girlfriend. God was not at the center of my life. Often times I put Him first in thought, but not always in actions. I would pray first thing upon waking up and even have devotion every morning. After this, I would go about my day. This was my interpretation of putting God first at the time.

"Putting God first" is having a true relationship with Him; and this means that He is not only the priority in your life, He is at the core of your life and every single thought, decision, and action revolves around Him. He is whom you should consult before engaging in every action regarding life. I didn't consult with Him before deciding to date my ex. I prayed but prayer consisted of telling Him what I was going to do and asking Him to bless it rather than listening. When God is put first it is full surrender, allowing Him full access as captain of your ship to have total control over your life.

In my previous relationship with God, I would convince myself that He was first in my life because I started every morning with prayer; however, that is where I went wrong. God could not have been the captain of my ship while I was still trying to control the helm.

> *Everything could be so beautiful. If only we would wait and trust in God instead of being impulsive and impatient and allowing the devil to play matchmaker for us.*

I loved and loved blindly. While we were dating, we were impulsive, impractical and impatient, and as a result, we cordially invited lust into our relationship. Satan was able to ruin two lives in one shot. Lust is everything short of the real thing. I could never give what I didn't have. I could never be who I didn't know. Also, not totally recovered from my past, I could never heal by being in another relationship. Meanwhile, Christ was persistently and patiently asking me to yield to Him.

This experience was my final attempt at dating. I had had enough! I walked away from dating and never looked back. You too may have the desire to reflect, reminisce and look back on what you lost. Even if all you have are cold memories, you can look to Christ and receive more love than you may ever want. By His grace I can write these words. I've lived and learned. I've asked for forgiveness and I'm a better man.

Wintered Memories

She sat there in darkness and void.
Off the edge of his heart.
Head down. Eyes stained.
Waiting there for the morning.
Hoping he would notice her.
If only he would...
Stop for a moment to
embrace her with his
attention.
Embrace her with his intentions.
Only if ... would he
permit her warm to
flood into nakedness.
He would notice the reason the
corners of him shriveled cold.

All left of her now
was the frigid shadow of her memory.
By the time he decided to love her
without qualms, it was too late.
Her once-fluid and tender heart hardened
in the absence of his touch
broke away in the emptiness of his love.

Regardless of which character you are in this poem, there is a God full of grace and truth who knows what it feels like to be unloved. He knows the feeling of hurt, despair, and loneliness. He also loves you with a deep compassion and an undying love. Anyone with faith and longing for His love can find comfort and peace within His embrace; within the tenderness of His incomparable embrace, all who are heavy laden may find rest. "Come unto me, all ye that labor and are heavy laden, and I will give you rest."[2]

> *I bet you thought it was a good idea:*
>
> *He or she possessed half of the qualities you were searching for in a mate. So you thought you would settle temporarily, and in time try to change him or her. However, understand this, you cannot change anyone. Time doesn't even always change people. You are too beautiful to settle for less than you deserve. Leave the matching-making to God. The more you try to make something work that isn't supposed to, the more you may be setting yourself and the person you are dating up for nothing but hurt and devastation in the end.*

---

[2] Matthew 11:28

Hopeless Promises

You promised me I reminded you of forever.
You never walked into anything with your whole heart.
Your ex was the perfect imperfectionist.

Clumsy like you with your emotions.
Breaking everything he put his hands on.
I trusted you were healed from it all.

I estimated this conclusion by time.
But realized, sometimes time can instigate the time to heal.
In my mind, the clapping of your two heels.

As your silhouette grows smaller and smaller.
Not sure if I'm going through a breakup or breakdown.
You always walked out of things with your whole heart.

You were never any good at keeping promises.

What Every Woman Needs to know About Men

I've seen women being stalked by exes who hollowed their hearts. They are martyrs for love. Left dead to trust again, to love, or even to cry or sing again.

Suicidal raindrop cry dragging around like a pulseless trust. The more she pulls, the more he pushes her away.

The more he tries, she pushes him away.

The word *love* is traumatizing. To these women, I cannot say I know what it feels like to be used and tossed around from men to men, but I've been on both sides of infidelity. I've been hurt before and done the hurting. Played, lied and lied to, cheated and cheated on. I could've allowed it to ruin me; to rip me like tears to the sole. But I sought after Jesus. He fixed me.

He loves you. He created you. He will do you no harm but only good all the days of your life. No man can hurt you in His arms, and no man can or will love you like He does. To the brokenhearted, come back. We miss you. We love you. This world is very dark without your smile.

The Most Beautiful Arrangement of Broken II

It seems as if many men love to talk about the broken woman as if men aren't broken; when in all actuality, it's the "broken man" that made the "broken woman" so popular.

To the broken women who may be reading this, I dedicate this to you. There is nothing wrong with being broken. We all have our different degrees of brokenness. You may be a scattered work of art, longing to recognize your own beauty. You may be broken, yet still, you are beautiful.[3]

The quote, "There is nothing wrong with being broken," can be misinterpreted without reading *The Most Beautiful Arrangement of Broken* in its entirety. There is something wrong with being broken, but the point that I'm attempting to convey is that there isn't anything wrong with admitting to the fact that you are broken. If you are broken and reading this, there is a side of you the world will never comprehend. It's because he has but one perception of you.

---

[3] Sean L. Brereton, *The Most Beautiful Arrangement of Broken,* (New York: Sean L. Brereton Books, 2015), i.

One is really two: Either too strong to be broken or too broken to be strong. So without pondering your disposition or a dash of compassion, the world would either batter you with expectations then refer to you as inferior or incompetent without successfully meeting those expectations. Or disregard your ability to be strong and take full advantage of your weakened condition. There's only one Man strong enough to mend your beautiful broken pieces and that is Christ the Savior.

Redefinition of a Man

A real man would never take advantage of a broken woman. He wouldn't only contact her when he needed her. He wouldn't use her and discard her when he didn't need her, nor would he stand by and watch her take advantage of herself. If he knew his role, he would celebrate her worth. You are priceless. Brokenness doesn't equate to weakness or uselessness. In fact, you are not as helpless as this may make you seem. He broke you because he's broken. He thought breaking you would fix him. You are gold. Your scars represent long suffering. Wear them like a tiger.

Before ending this section, I need to address the broken men. Society depicts men to be unbreakable and when a man exhibits any type of emotion, he is labeled as weak.

One of the worst things that can happen to a man is a breakup. We may even suffer from depression after the demand to readjust to a life as a single man and without the companionship of someone who we grew to love. Women hurt men more often than we publicize; and there isn't anything wrong with a man crying over a breakup. It's customary for men to appear to be strong outwardly, while inside he is suffering. Yes, God created men to be strong, resilient leaders, so I'm not saying that it's okay for a man to be a crybaby and bawling down the place every second... While it is true that many of the prophets were bold, courageous and manly, these biblical heroes also cried; Jeremiah is one in particular who comes to mind. Nevertheless, I am speaking to the idea perpetuated by society that men don't cry, that men don't get hurt, and that men don't need love and affection.

If you're hurting and in need of social support, it's better to let your closest friends know instead of hiding it. Cry out to God and seek Him as a Helper. He will comfort and console you when you're hurting when the world thinks you are too strong to be hurt.

LOVE ME BACK

I showed you nothing but love.
I am not valued by you.
I cannot stay here any longer.
I can't force you to love me back.

DEADLY ALIVE

I've seen you treated like
bathroom stalls.
Depraved.
We corrupt society.
Slaughter your purity.
Mock you.
Now you try to break the day with
a broken smile.
Your muffled hymn stare.
Imprisoning the church inside of you.
You wear an introverted cloak for

a covering,
concealing pain like a weapon.

Once ready to feel without killing.
Now ready to kill without feeling.

Smile no longer soft, but shell-like cave.
Left like an allegory for death.
Write like an oxymoron for life.
Beneath it all, I know
you're still beautiful.
Beneath it all,
I know the devil is just borrowing you
for a moment.
I know God still watches over your corpse
raining teardrops,
soaking grace and mercy in his eyes.
Beneath the grim shadow of your past,
beneath the stench of death, and behind
the police tape,
I know you're still
alive.

Regarding love and the affairs of our hearts, the missing ingredient is timing. An army of broken hearts would not be roaming the earth if we would wait on God's timing. Everything can be beautiful, especially when both persons are healed from their pasts and ready to trust and love again. Consequently, we miss out on a healthy future when we maintain an unhealthy past—we need to discontinue feeding of something that should've died a long time ago. Don't continue to add gloom to your future. Always move forward—it is the only direction that is relevant. Despite these words, some will still give in to passion. I get it! It feels amazing to be loved. But some close their eyes and open their hearts and give themselves away too easily. For this reason, dating is more accepted—it is easier and less work. Men, women, you shouldn't expect someone else to properly care for your heart. The outer wounds may heal quickly but the internal wounds may stay for years.

Have you ever had a bad breakup? What were some of the things you experienced?

___

What are some things you could have done differently to end the relationship in a more cordial manner?

___

_____
_____
_____
_____
_____
_____
_____

Did you forgive your ex partner? Yes or no.

Did you forgive yourself? Yes or no.

Chapter 4
Recovering from Abuse

After a trying day at work, I walked home in the bitter cold, thinking today unlike most days I cannot wait to get home. My achy feet didn't help to relieve my situation as leaves were being tossed in the angry wind and the sky frowned as pregnant clouds continued to restrain the impatient rain. I thought about the welfare of the children at the school in which I worked. That day, they had challenged me. Disobedience, screaming, kicking, temper-tantrums are all just a snippet of the headache that I'm talking about. It was total onslaught. I thought about the children and the rest of the world's condition and was instantly saddened. Suddenly all I heard was, "You B-word!" I looked to my left and about ten feet away was a man arguing with a woman. "Great!" I muttered under my breath. I hated to see women disrespected. Even worse, the couple's body language exposed to me the notion that this was a domestic violence situation. He verbally insulted her and got in her face. He would do this then continue walking. When she responded, he repeated his actions. This happened about four times and each time it seemed as if he got closer to hitting her. I walked in the ugly cold despising that horrid scene. The leaves smacking around the air furiously around me apparently shared my empathy.

By now, the unruly couple had kept straight on their path and left me to turn the corner on route to my home. But something in me couldn't walk away. I kept looking back until I decided to turn around and follow them. I thought if he was confrontational with me, I would defend her or myself or both. At the same time as I began to follow them, he suddenly began to speed up, leaving her behind him to catch up.

Now about twenty feet behind her, I walked speedily to catch up; Fifteen, ten, at five feet away I inquired of her, "Excuse me...are you okay?" She turned around shocked, hurt, embarrassed and with eyes dampened in sorrow and replied, "Yes."

I Know How to Handle Him

"Do you want me to pray for you?" I asked. She declared, "Yes!" I then told her hesitantly, "I'm not sure if right here right now is the best time or place, but I can later..." She looked ahead to make sure her aggressive guy friend was still walking ahead and didn't look back to see her talking to me. The reluctance in her eyes showed me she too didn't think now was a good idea, as. Instead I took her Facebook information and walked with her, breaking the silence after about two minutes. "You know you don't have to live like that right? "You don't have to allow him or any man to treat you that way." "I know how to handle him," she insisted. "Oh?" I was unconvinced by her words. Not too long, we arrived at her destination. I told her, "God bless you!" and continued on my journey home.

"I know how to handle him." Her words replayed in my mind. I thought to myself, if you truly did, you wouldn't allow him to curse you out in public while possibly assaulting you in private. Is this how some women living in the bondage of an abusive relationship think? I posit that these women and men—yes, men are also victims of emotional, verbal, physical and sexual abuse—are victims of mind control. Why not run away or shout out for help? Why go back and live in these situations? Abused individuals are normally entrapped by fear. The abusive partner, either male or female, instills fear by threatening to hurt and in some cases murder his or her partner., or even—One would think separation is a good thing in cases like these but to these victims, life without their abusers is worse than life with them.

There is a route of escape. You don't have to live in fear. I know of a personal story where someone living with an abusive boyfriend escaped. She confided in an older friend from her church who insisted she get the police and her parents involved. By the grace of God, she escaped unharmed and had a restraining order issued against her boyfriend. She was finally able to live in peace and never had to deal with or see her abuser's face again. If you are in an abusive relationship, remember that God is your protection. Cry out to Him. Ask Him for deliverance and strength. "Trust in the Lord with all your heart and lean not unto your own understanding" (Proverbs 3:5). Tell someone! Seek professional and police help and confide in a trustworthy friend or family member. There are domestic violence hotlines you can also call to aid in your situation.

GONE FOR GOOD

No matter how shadow the dusk of my day,
his moonlight is always smiling.
Could access my Milky Way, but he
wanted to wait till after the wedding day.
His comet eyes staring like a
sweet brook.
Downstream.
Could lie in his arms till midnight.
Not a player like the rest of them.
Never was impressed by them.
No bathroom break phone calls.
Meeting up with "thots" on IG.
Hitting on and beating me.
He was a scripture-chanting,
commandment-keeping,
man of God.
Waited too long.
Seen all the fakes before...
This is real.
But I have to break him.
Better pray for him.
Pray God protects him from what I'm about to do.
For me, fidelity is a doctrine of mythology.
It's like second nature, being cheated on.
So I'm on cheating.
He should've come earlier.
Too late for any guy to be good
in my eyes. Deceased to it.
I was already gone forbad.

Don't build a home on top of a landfill and then complain about the stench. The more you allow it, the more you make the both of you comfortable.

Sometimes you make it easier for both of you to settle in the filth of his mistreatment by continuing to allow it. You deserve better than a stagnant and unfruitful relationship. God won't have you rot in the mistreatment of someone who can't appreciate your worth. Let go, and find comfort in the hands of God.

I Prayed for You

It was so real,
those episodes,
sinking courtships.
Legally blind dates.
Kept thinking, maybe this time...
I'm not trying to imply that
I didn't love life, but I was
barren like Hannah,
praying to
one day see God's hand in my
love life.
Tear gas seeping from the pain
in my agony,
giving me a
drunken demeanor.
All I wanted was to conceive love.
Nightfall on those fall nights
is when it hit me.
I was on a stroll in a euphoric garden where

everything was good.
But this garden
was the most
beautiful ugly.
Just wanted to fit in.
But I couldn't find companionship
among an obnoxious company of beasts.
Then I would wake up
to a
daydream of your
footprints on my heart.
It's only been endless eons I've
been petitioning with God for the
radiance of your smile to
brighten my life.
So I'm not saying I believe in
soul mates, but when God mates souls,
the end product is soul mates.
You are the yes
to the question that marks
itself shamelessly in the corners of my
prayer box.

This is surreal. I prayed for you.

Pray For Healing

Another important thing to pray for, even before moving on from a bad relationship, is restoration. Healing is vital for your own well-being, and if you're considering exclusive dating, you must first be healed from the emotional baggage of the past in order to move forward.

Every so often, nostalgia creeps up on us and rubs away all the reasons we ended a relationship. We should never allow feelings to obscure our good judgment.

> *You were sunny and beautiful. You were moving on and doing fine.*

Old things die so that new things can grow. Your breakup doesn't mean your life is over. Where new growth can take place, new adventures can be shared, deeper love can be experienced, and new life can begin.

> *She wanted to skip the disappointment and rejection. She wanted to fast-forward from anxiety to anniversary, from heartbreak to a happy ending. He played the game. He wanted to skip the bases and win without work. They were both hoping to find the cheat codes for love.*

From time to time, we are bold and impatient and wander outside of God's plan for instant, effortless, and convenient love. After acquiring your quick and easy love, you realize that there are no cheat codes for love. Then the relationship fails, and you're left emotionally distraught. You need to take some time to heal. The person you thought you could trust may come back around. When he does, please do not entertain him. Leave him alone. Respect the condition of your healing.

God is a Healer

Christians, I do not mean to sound insensitive, but we've all been hurt before. Take some time to heal by spending it with the ultimate healer. "Jesus saith unto him, I am the way, the truth, and the life: no man cometh unto the Father, but by me."[4]

Every time you interrupt your healing process by entering into another relationship, you make it worse for yourself spiritually and emotionally. Don't rip off the Band-Aid God put on you and allow germs to enter the wound. . Stop. Allow God to heal you first before making yourself available for love again. .

As you heal, don't allow your breakup to define you. See it as a learning experience and an opportunity to start fresh. Though right now may not be the right time, don't give up on hope. There are good and faithful men out there who will love you—all of you. However, don't allow your desire for companionship to distract you from the most important relationship you can ever have.

Instead of waiting for the right person, ask God if courtship is in His will for you, and if so, ask him to prepare you to be the right person and show you the right time.

You cannot permit yourself to be so blinded by passion that you miss your stop. While getting to know someone, stay focused enough to jump out of the situation if it is going in a direction you're not comfortable going in. Never be led to

---

[4] John 14:6

compromise your standards and undermine your non-negotiables. No person is worth losing yourself over. That person is simply not the one for you.

> *If I give you my time, it's because I think you are special and worthy of it. The minute you start to take me for granted, and start to believe that I deserve second-class treatment, we can easily go right back to the day before you existed.*

As mentioned earlier, I support forgiveness. However, I am intolerant of emotional abuse. The aftereffects of abuse are very harmful and may be long-term. After the relationship has ended, if you have forgiven the person who hurt you and are comfortable being friends with him or her, make it very clear that you have moved on and have absolutely no interest in a future relationship. In a pleasant way, let him or her know you are not the scorned and broken man or woman he or she might expect you to be; that you have risen above it and have genuinely forgiven him or her. However, maintaining a friendship after a relationship has ended is not easy for most and not usually recommended. Leave your past alone, because you are building on your future with your present.

> *Cut all ties with your past. Before new growth can begin, the split ends must be clipped.*

This means absolutely no communication, face-to-face or virtually. Removing yourself and disconnecting from an ex's social media account(s) may also be beneficial. Without the distraction of emotions that will hinder your recovery, you can focus on God and yourself. Then you can rediscover who you are as an individual for yourself and others and for whoever may be the next one to love you.

A Dying Relationship

HOLDING ON

Holding on for dear life.
We dangle.
Sitting uncomfortably.
In the crevice.
I,

holding on for dear's life.
She, breathe in me.
These, angry tears
running. From my shirt,
from the edge
of my pledge
to hold on no matter
how hard it got.
How solid heart cold.

We contradicted.
Still, you found a way to be lung.
Still found a way to let our
bloody memories air-dry.
You call it art.
I see vanity.
This accident disfigured our future.

DATING VS. COURTSHIP

Now, here we are.
Decorating the side of this mount.
Sun smoking our backs.
Melting the candles we once lit
and vowed to praise forever.
Now rocks crying out 'cause
we can't burn in these rays forever.
If I let go, we die, but
right now, death is a *lifeline*.
Now, I line my life up with my fear of heights.
Before you.
To fall for you.
That's why I was a fool
to trip on this road with my
stationary faith.
Like this, we car with no gas.
Plant in the cleft of this rock.
We cliffhangers!

At ten years old, I loved road trips.
Every ten minutes: are we there yet?
Now realize after all these years,
we still not there yet.
We still not there.
We still not.
We still.
We.

> *I know it's like staring death in the face, but it's time to let go (of this relationship).*

"Trust in the Lord with all thine heart; and lean not unto thine own understanding."[5]

If you are enduring a dead relationship, there isn't anything good about you allowing a man or woman's bad habits to taint your perception of love. And you don't need to stay around long enough to rot in anyone's bad habits.

Too Comfortable

You gave him everything
you had and he never appreciated it.
He never understood the depth of your
stubborn love for him because no one has ever
believed in him. No one has ever loved him as hard
as you did. Although you've grown comfortable in his bed
of sloppy lies and clumsy, inconsistent love, you can't stay. It's
time to wake up and make the bed. You have overstayed
your welcome.

Clock Games and Brick Doors

You ain't playing hard to get.
Just don't want to waste any more time.
You know what pain feels like,
know the feeling of that slicing
sand rushing through your glass pipe.
Who told them they could destroy you?
Who told them you would enjoy it?

You know what it feels like for love to be nothing more than

---

[5] Proverbs 3:5–6

a casual church bell echo
ringing off a man's lips
like spit. She's
sick
of it so much she threw up
fist. Love is a salesman with
a lisp.
Tap dancing on the heart of your door.
After you finally open up to him, he's gone.
Gone, after taking all of what he brought
in with him, with a piece of you too.
While leaving all of his trash behind.

So if you do not text back right away
or at all, if you've grown bricks to
keep him from getting too close,
you're saying you've read poems
like him before.
That has a bite much worse than its bark.
He must be real, genuine.
Honest as a bell tower.
Show you this time he's serious.
Leave the games and his shoes
at the door.

    Men, you are called to be kings; and women, you should never forget how much of a timeless queen you are. As women, you sometimes seek comfort in companionship at the expense of your growth, standards, and morals. Is it really worth it to continue to be in a relationship when it's costing you so much to elevate him? Men too compromise their standards and beliefs and settle for someone they should not be with. Wasted time is an expense you cannot afford.

Ladies, every man who is interested in a relationship with you needs to understand that you are tired of the men who played with your heart. You do not want or need to waste anymore time! You have an ensemble of bachelors throwing their shameless advances at you. Yet the ones who didn't appreciate you are still calling and text-messaging you, sorry about being sorry for how they've treated you. They say, "You don't know what you have until it's gone." I say, "He knew what he had. He just didn't realize how much of it had him." There are good guys out there who are not interested in playing games and trifling with your heart. He is somewhere waiting and praying for you. Gentlemen, there are women out there who are beautiful inside and out, waiting for someone who will take love seriously.

To trifle with hearts is a crime of no small magnitude in the sight of a holy God. And yet some will show preference for young ladies, call out their affections, and then go their way and forget all about the words they have spoken and their effect. A new face attracts them, and they repeat the same words, devote the same attention to another. This disposition will reveal itself in married life. The marriage relation does not always make the fickle mind firm, the wavering steadfast and true to principle. They tire of constancy, and unholy thoughts will manifest themselves in unholy actions.[6]

---

[6] Ellen G. White, *Letters to Young Lovers* (Pacific Press Publishing Association, 1984), 74.

You already know what hurt feels like and do not need any more examples. Your pursuer must be patient, compassionate, sincere, and honest. This man or woman must show you that he or she is serious with your time, or they must leave.

I'm sure you can be in a relationship but you should be confident enough to know you cannot and will not be with just anyone. You are tired of the dating game. You are waiting for the one you've been praying for and will not give your body to anyone but the person you will be married to. This thinking does not equate to conceit or playing hard to get. It means that you just refuse to settle. I'm also sure you want to be intimate and affectionate with someone at this very moment; however, you must be familiar with the equivalence of your worth. Do not settle. Even if you've made some mistakes in the past, learn to value your body and your heart. They belong to a nurturing God who sees all and won't permit you to be in a relationship that will draw you away from Him.

If you keep giving out free samples, you won't have much for the one you don't need to convince.

Chapter 5
Dating vs. Courtship

Some of you may be thinking what the big deal with courtship is and why is it relevant to me today.? You may even be thinking that courtship is outdated while dating is the modern thing. Others may be asking themselves if it is possible to follow God's plan under the dating headline. Some, if not all, of these questions may be bombarding your mind; and I get it. Although there's no evil in thinking these things, as I walk you through some points, I warn all to be careful while carefully considering the big deal or difference between courtship and dating.

Christians are warned in 1 Peter 5:8 to "be sober, be vigilant" and in Matthew 10:16 to "be wise as serpents, and harmless as doves." It isn't a long time in which new believers come to an understanding that:

> "For every lawful, God-given privilege, Satan has a counterfeit to suggest. The holy, pure thought he seeks to replace with the impure. For the sanctity of married love he would substitute with permissiveness, unfaithfulness, excess, and

perversion; premarital sex, adultery, animalism in and outside of marriage, and homosexuality."

What this quote means is Satan, the roaring lion, is deceptive. He is also as cunning in his entrancements as when he deceived our first parents, Adam and Eve, into falling into sin. If you can manufacture any inanition product well enough to resemble the real thing, you can get away with murder. Bootleggers and counterfeit artists understand this idea well.

Pinpointing the Counterfeit

The infamous Canal Street of New York City is well-known for producing thousands of counterfeit products, many of which are known by the masses to be the imitation versions. But there are also many who rarely discern the difference between the real and counterfeit versions. Additionally, there are those con artists who hastily replicate tickets, selling them at a cheaper price, whenever top artists have concerts in major cities. Unaware, some innocent consumer purchases a ticket or two, waits in line for hours in the blistering cold or scorching sun, only to be gravely disappointed and heartbroken when they are rejected for attempting to gain access to the concert with an unauthentic ticket. How would you feel if this were you? I know I would be pissed off. I also would be more vigilant and think twice before making certain purchases—not that I go to concerts anyway. Why then are we not equally invested in matters of our hearts?

I am definitely not the first to come to the conclusion that dating is Satan's counterfeit for God's ideal. In order to better understand this thought, we must consider what God's ideal is. "For I know the thoughts that I think toward you, saith the LORD, thoughts of peace, and not of evil, to give you an expected end" (Jeremiah 29:11). God's ideal for every person is happiness and holiness. "Because it is written: Be ye holy; for I am holy" (1 Peter 1:16) and "These things have I spoken unto you, that my joy might remain in you, and that your joy might be full" (John 15:11).

This vehement desire for us equally concerns those who He calls into marriage. Paul penned God's goal for marriage in Ephesians 5:22-27,

> "Wives, submit yourselves unto your own husbands, as unto the Lord. For the husband is the head of the wife, even as Christ is the head of the church: and he is the savior of the body. Therefore as the church is subject unto Christ, so let the wives be to their own husbands in everything. Husbands, love your wives, even as Christ also loved the church, and gave himself for it; That he might sanctify and cleanse it with the washing of water by the word, That he might present it to himself a glorious church, not having spot, or wrinkle, or any such thing; but that it should be holy and without blemish."

When contemplating dating, or as some may call it, "the dating game", it is important to ponder what the end result is. By God's grace some do survive the dating game and are now happily married; again, I say, by God's grace. Now whether out of ignorance for what God wanted or not, these individuals still took a risk.

I am one of those people. I never understood the difference between courtship and dating until a couple of years ago; I can admit that even if I plainly understood the difference, I would've still resorted to dating. I was defiant back then. If it were not for God's mercy, things could've been horrendous for me. Whether we are oblivious to God's path or not, we may still suffer from the ramifications of our actions. There are things I did and said to people that I cannot take back.

Christ said, "The Lord is not slack concerning his promise, as some men count slackness; but is longsuffering to us-ward, not willing that any should perish, but that all should come to repentance" (2 Peter 3:9). This is God's ultimate desire; but ultimately, many will perish by choice. Furthermore, how many men and women, boys and girls are perishing emotionally?

Dating vs. God's Commandments

When considering God's Decalogue, how many of His commandments are disregarded and obliterated in the dating model? Let's run through each commandment and reflect on that question:

i. Thou shalt have no other gods before me.
ii. Thou shalt not make unto thee any graven image, or any likeness of anything that is in heaven above, or that is in the earth beneath, or that is in the water under the earth.
iii. Thou shalt not bow down thyself to them, nor serve them: for I the Lord thy God am a jealous God, visiting the iniquity of the fathers upon the children unto the third and fourth generation of

them that hate me; And shewing mercy unto thousands of them that love me, and keep my commandments.

iv. Thou shalt not take the name of the Lord thy God in vain; for the Lord will not hold him guiltless that taketh his name in vain.

v. Remember the sabbath day, to keep it holy. Six days shalt thou labour, and do all thy work: But the seventh day is the sabbath of the Lord thy God: in it thou shalt not do any work, thou, nor thy son, nor thy daughter, thy manservant, nor thy maidservant, nor thy cattle, nor thy stranger that is within thy gates: For in six days the Lord made heaven and earth, the sea, and all that in them is, and rested the seventh day: wherefore the Lord blessed the sabbath day, and hallowed it.

vi. Honour thy father and thy mother: that thy days may be long upon the land which the Lord thy God giveth thee.

vii. Thou shalt not kill.

viii. Thou shalt not commit adultery.

ix. Thou shalt not steal.

x. Thou shalt not bear false witness against thy neighbour.

xi. Thou shalt not covet thy neighbour's house, thou shalt not covet thy neighbor's wife, nor his manservant, nor his maidservant, nor his ox, nor his ass, nor any thing that is thy neighbour's.

—Exodus 20:3-17

Written by the hand of God yet made so ineffective in typical dating, how?

Commandment no. 1, "Thou shalt have no other gods before me." The unguarded passions feed into infatuation and have the potential to push some to idolize their partners— a practice that isn't limited to dating. But courtship follows certain principles to guard against infatuation.

Commandment no. 3, "Thou shalt not take the name of the Lord thy God in vain." When we call ourselves Christians or children of God yet act contrary to the high and holy name we bear and His character, we take His name in vain. We "deny the power thereof" (2 Timothy 3:5).

Commandment no. 4, "Remember the Sabbath day to keep it holy." The Sabbath is a beautiful time to spend with God and the people you love. In typical dating or to be fair, even in courtship, ask yourself, does this relationship help me to keep God's Sabbath hours holy?

Commandment no. 5, "Honour thy father and thy mother: that thy days may be long upon the land which the LORD thy God giveth thee." In many respects this commandment is undermined when romantic couples see each other behind their parents' backs. In some cases, relationships continue even after the mother or father's disapproval of a romantic partner.

Commandment no 6, "Thou shalt not kill." Because of careless behaviors in dating, we are killing ourselves and others mentally and emotionally.

Commandment no. 7, "Thou shalt not commit adultery." Sexual sin is customary in dating. It's also very possible to occur in courtship. Though there is a Biblical difference between adultery and fornication, both are grossly sinful and offensive to God. Premarital sex tends to be promoted more in dating. Kissing, cuddling, groping, sexting, masturbating, oral/anal sex are not exceptions (the last two acts are dishonorable to God outside and within marriage). All of these things cross the forbidden and regrettable boundary of physical, mental and emotional intimacy.

Commandment no. 8, "Thou shalt not steal." Those who choose to date may steal the heart, affections and intimacy of their partner. Flirtation is practiced, feelings are aroused and boundaries are crossed until the seventh commandment is not heeded. Also, parents are dishonored here.

Commandment no. 9, "Thou shalt not bear false witness against thy neighbour." Under the intoxicating influence of emotions and while jumping in and out of romantic situations that aren't necessarily relationships, the temptation to lie is more prominent. Some cheat and lie to prevent themselves from getting caught. Also, a bad habit of slandering the name of a former partner is practiced in case where we allow our emotions to rule us.

Commandment no. 10, "Thou shalt not covet thy neighbor's property". When misery and pain are induced through an accumulation of treacherous blows to the heart and insensitive disappointments, you may begin to look at seemingly happy couples and covet, wanting what they have.

Lying and coveting, as well as the others may be present in courtship as well as dating. However, through a thorough system of steps, courtship better enables you to honor and glorify God. It is designed to help you and your partner better resemble God's character.

This profound quote from *The Adventist Home* puts these thoughts into perspective:

The ideas of courtship have their foundation in erroneous ideas concerning marriage. They follow impulse and blind passion. The courtship is carried on in a spirit of flirtation. The parties frequently violate the rules of modesty and reserve and are guilty of indiscretion, if they do not break the law of God. The high, noble, lofty design of God in the institution of marriage is not discerned; therefore, the purest affections of the heart, the noblest traits of character are not developed.

Do not misunderstand this quote. It is not discouraging courtship but addressing the fact that there is a right and wrong way to carry out courtship. The devil did not stop at introducing the counterfeit dating, he also perverted true courtship. Was he not the first liar in all existence? Christ answers this question in a rebuke to the Pharisees,

> "Ye are of your father the devil, and the lusts of your father ye will do. He was a murderer from the beginning, and abode not in the truth, because there is no truth in him. When he speaketh a lie, he speaketh of his own: for he is a liar, and the father of it" (John 8:44).

This same father of lies, whose downfall began in heaven, Lucifer said, "I will ascend above the heights of the clouds; I will be like the Most High" (Isaiah 14:14). He coveted after God's kingdom. He hated righteousness. He despised God's commandments, which are an expression of His character. Therefore, in Satan's counterfeit or perverted system of courtship, these same character traits of covetousness and contempt for God's commandments will be manifested.

God is Not the Author of Situationships

Whether we are dating, courting, married or single, we need to ask Christ to help us to be contrary to Satan and be more like God, daily! Dating makes more room for complication. Ever heard of the term *situationship*? Satan is the father of lies, dating is the father of situationships. A situationship is a relationship that is not going anywhere. There may be lots of physical intimacy but little to no commitment. A definite title for the relationship may be absent while emotions and passion runs wildly. The questions that arise out of these types of situations are usually, What are we? Are we together or not? We do everything like a couple, when are we going to make things official? Whatever behaviors exist within a situationship, positive or negative, there is little happiness but much confusion.

"God is not the author of confusion" (1 Corinthians 14:33); He wants "all things to be done decently and in order" (1 Corinthians 14:40). This command does not exclude romance; there is nothing decent or orderly about how dating is conducted. God wants no misery, pain or covetous spirit for us. He supplies all our needs once we seek first His kingdom and His righteousness (Matthew 6:33).

The Straight and Narrow Way

Can we agree that dating is the more popular and accepted practice? It is *wide* in its behavior and *broad* in its approach with few regulations and prohibitions. Christ proclaimed, "Enter ye in at the strait gate: for wide is the gate, and broad is the way, that leadeth` to destruction, and many there be which go in thereat: Because strait is the gate, and narrow is the way, which leadeth unto life, and few there be that find it" Matthew 7:14. While the majority of the world is consciously and unconsciously participating in dating, whose gate leads to destruction, very few are walking the straight and narrow path of courtship. Dating, to me, resembles a sort of test to see if something could grow from the scattered seeds of two destinies intertwined by a wind of interest. Courtship and dating both share an element of walking into the unknown—you may not necessarily be certain where the relationship may end up. However, courtship, straight and narrow in its approach, is built on trust in God. Those who date may attest to having faith in God, but the behavior in courtship demonstrates full faith and obedience in God, while dating is much more carefree having little emotional and physical and principles that are open to interpretation. Dating is risky because people tend to date in order to get to know each other. This is dangerous because you've already agreed to make yourself emotionally, mentally, and in many cases physically vulnerable before having adequate information about the person you're dating. Intimacy tends to come before commitment.

While dating, if you discover undesirable character traits in a person, uncontrolled hormones usually make it harder to end the relationship. In courtship, barriers are set up to prevent you from becoming too emotionally involved and attached too soon; its design to protect you makes it safer than dating.

A farmer doesn't scatter seeds randomly and hope for a plentiful harvest. He or she researches the quality of the soil, testing its pH for nutrient content, and considers the environment and climate of the farmland. What is the content and environment of your potential relationship? Do you have practical and substantial reasons to consider a young man or woman as a potential partner? Would you consider him as a genuine friend? Is your friendship rooted in Christ? Is He the Sower of your love? You should not make the decision to court someone unless there is sufficient information available about the candidate; but ultimately, the decision is yours whether you are faithful to the courtship process.

Nevertheless, even while being prayerful, the devil will still make grave attempts to deceive those who think God is leading them—even in courtship; even while being in the world but not of the world.

You, as a child of God are called to be different from the world. God identifies His own as, "a chosen generation, a royal priesthood, an holy nation, a peculiar people" (1 Peter 2:9).

God's children are the apple of His eye (Psalm 17:8) and whether you are a Christian or not, you too can have a better and more fruitful love experience. God has a higher standard for His people and through His people wants to impart it to the world. While I pen these thoughts, I'd like to caution you, whether you are a follower of Christ or not, you shouldn't attempt to enjoy the fruit of following these principles solely for a better love life. You should want better for yourself, not just to reap the benefits of God's goodness but to get to know Him and love Him.

There is no particular formula for Christian courtship in the Bible. Every Biblical courtship was unique; but once we really understand God's ideal and desire for His own, any practice or behavior contrary to achieving His best should be avoided. Let's see if you can name the practice, either courtship or dating, based on the behavior? The answers will be provided at the end of the chapter.

Dating vs. Courtship Quiz

Fill in the blanks

1. _____usually happens when the timing is right. This timing is when the candidates are both old enough to understand the physical, emotional, and spiritual demands of love and marriage and be able to act accordingly, by God's grace.

2. _____usually happens when either a man or woman or both are lonely, an attraction is sparked or verbalized, or whenever the opportunity presents itself.

3. _____ tends to happen after schooling is completed.

4. _____usually occurs whenever emotions are fired up and hormones are feverish. Beginning at the high school years and now even as early as middle school. Youngsters who have no idea what they are involving themselves into are _____.

5._____ observes or should observe physical and emotional boundaries.

DATING VS. COURTSHIP

6._____ is not always, but usually is carefree and tends to have no physical and emotional barriers. If you love/like your partner enough, even premarital sex is customary.

7._____ is designed to end without leaving either person heartbroken, depressed and with bitter resentment for their ex-partner.

8._____ tends to end in disappointment, heartbreak and misery.

9._____ is designed to help you acknowledge and care for your partner as a child of God. It promotes loving selflessly. Love, primarily for God and then for your special friend is recognized and exercised.

10._____ usually encourages lust. If you want it, take it. If it feels good, do it.

11. _____ is designed to happen only after God reveals that marriage is in you and your partner's will and you both are ready for marriage.

12._____ usually doesn't wait on God's directions.

13. In _____, if you're not careful you can rush into things and be left full of regret and shame.

14._____ helps you understand the importance of patience. _____ helps you understand that real love develops slowly.

If you refuse courtship and would rather date instead, at least keep these two things at the forefront of your mind:

> *Don't rush into relationships, and don't rush in relationships.*

Take things slowly, and really get to know one another. Avoid all types of temptation, including placing yourself in a position to take things too far. I'm sure you may be anxious, and the connection you two share will be strong. It will also be very soothing to feel his touch or stare, but set safe boundaries, and know your limits. Also, don't put yourself in a position to be pressured or manipulated into doing things that you're uncomfortable doing or not ready to do, such as having sexual intercourse or engaging in any action or idea that may lead up to the act of intercourse. Love doesn't work that way. Honestly contemplate whether you two can grow together. Never confuse lust for love. Lastly, glorify God in all that you do and pray before making decisions.

Answers to Dating Vs. Courtship Quiz

1. Courtship
2. Dating
3. Courtship
4. Dating, dating
5. Courtship
6. Dating
7. Courtship
8. Dating
9. Courtship
10. Dating
11. Courtship
12. Dating
13. Dating
14. Courtship, courtship

Chapter 6
Help from the Experts

Besides the fact that many individuals are dangerously impulsive regarding the dating scene, many are indecisive. People indulge in flirtatious and deceptive relations and seem to find pleasure in leading other people on. A similar sentiment expressed in *The Adventist Home* is mentioned earlier, "Courtship, as carried on in this age, is a scheme of deception and hypocrisy...". Dr. Alanzo H. Smith also writes in *Why Good Relationships Turn Bad* that

One may be amazed at the different tactics people employ in order to form or maintain a relationship. Our research shows that men primarily use these tactics to gain sexual favors, while women use them to form or keep a relationship. The aim in forming a relationship should not be to win at all costs; the end does not justify the means... A relationship should not be formed based on just the material... Second, a relationship should not be formed on deceit.

After these suggestions, the following questions are recommended at the beginning stages of friendship before entering into a romantic relationship:

1. Are you married?
2. Do you have children?
3. If so what are their ages?
4. Are you working?
5. Are you divorced?
6. If so, are the divorced papers filed as yet?
7. On what grounds are you seeking a divorce?
8. How old are you?
9. Have you ever been in trouble with the law?
10. What is your level of education?
11. Do you have a fiancée?

Look for honesty and consistency in the answers to these questions and also in the actions of the person. The idea isn't to look for perfection but to always keep in mind that this could be the person who you may spend the rest of your life with. A union with this individual may have the greatest impact and influence than any other thing in your life. The late W.D. Frazee said it best, "Except to follow Christ, there is no decision that affects the total lifetime of a person more than life companionship."

I would advise all to neglect the obligation to consider who is right for you, and allow God and God alone to be your matchmaker. God matches people for eternity. I don't mean to imply that the relationship will last forever on Earth, but I suggest that the relationship will be edifying and of heavenly influence—your friendship can last eternally in heaven. Your partner should ensure your right to live forever and vice versa.

> *You do not need his protection.*
> *If he can't love you like you ought*
> *to be loved.*
> *He needs to uncage you,*
> *let you fly.*
> *To someone else*
> *you are a rainbow in the sky.*

Men, a woman needs to practice what she preaches. But we need to be accountable for our actions too. When a woman is loved, supported and knows that you want the relationship to work, she will give you her all. For the most part, the outcome of the relationship is dependant on your willingness.

Ladies, if a man says that he is willing to play his part in helping your relationship with him improve but doesn't show it, he is not ready for the relationship. Maybe he just doesn't want someone else to be with you. He keeps telling you that you are beautiful and smart and sexy, while you are everything but his committed partner. You may be thinking he's all there is. Set yourself free from where you are not appreciated and loved with his whole heart. You are someone else's perfect. Don't allow anyone to cage you in your insecurities. While he is telling you that you are black and white, someone else is trying to paint you in their sky!

The Fatal Attraction

It is my personal decision to refrain from dating. In this environment, the pressure to be attracted to the opposite sex is kindled. The excitement dating can bring may lead to the production of the hormone dopamine in your brain and create a desire to continue to engage with someone with whom you may only have a physical attraction. This may also lead to infatuation, or the act of "falling in love." Try not to "fall" in love; instead, make the decision to love based on the facts of the person's character and the reality of the person's personality. When we degrade love and reduce it to a mere feeling, we equate it to *catching feelings* and we end up loving people in romantic relationships that we have no business loving. In this practice, people become mated—consisting of two people who are not compatible, or suitable, and do not belong together—but *not* matched.

While the hormones serotonin and dopamine are active, they may cloud judgment and lead you to act impulsively and into situations that you may later come to regret. The pressure of dating may also cause feelings to develop before the reality of the person materializes. I believe some of the best relationships grow out of friendships. When you date, you allow a relationship to start before a friendship. If the relationship lasts, and you fall in love, this may be an impulsive love that lacks principle and discernment. However, the excuse, or reason, often given to continue on in a relationship is due to a neglect of intuition and the blind love that ignores signs that may be a cause for separation.

You never had to say it.
It reeks from you.
Don't want another guy to
treat you better
than he does.
You just want him to
treat you better
than he does.

The sad thing about love is that we often find ourselves emotionally involved with people who will never be good for us.

An unstable relationship is never good for us. It also implies that the circumstances will probably never change. While you are reading this, that house is up in flames. Grab your sanity and get out before it's too late! You do not walk out of a burning building; you run out. I know you want this relationship to last more than anything, but you should want to be happy more than anything.

Ellen G. White wrote something interesting in regard to this:

Few have correct views of the marriage relation. Many seem to think that it is the attainment of perfect bliss; but if they could know one quarter of the heartaches of men and women that are bound by the marriage vow in chains that they cannot and dare not break, they would not be surprised that I trace these lines. Marriage, in a majority of cases, is a most galling yoke. There are thousands that are mated but not matched. The books of heaven are burdened with the woes, the wickedness, and the abuse that lie hidden under the marriage mantle. This is why I would warn the young who are of a marriageable age to make haste slowly in the choice of a companion. The path of married life may appear beautiful and full of happiness; but why may not you be disappointed as thousands of others have been? Great care should be taken by Christian youth in the formation of friendships and in the choice of companions. Take heed, lest what you now think to be pure gold turns out to be base metal. Worldly associations tend to place obstructions in the way of your service to God, and many souls are ruined by unhappy unions, either business or matrimonial, with those who can never elevate or ennoble.[7]

If the relationship doesn't last, it is because the initial feelings begin to fade, and you finally get to discover who this stranger that you call your girlfriend/boyfriend or wife/husband really is.

Get acquainted with people in a natural social context. I encourage meeting new people and socializing with them. While you get to know them on a platonic level, diligently observe their characters and their personalities. Consider whether this man or woman has a character that is reputable and noble. Deem whether his influence and reason would encourage you to grow as an individual.

The XY Theory

Ladies, this adds another concern to the relationship scene. Another thing women should know is that both a man's character, along with his personality, should be taken into account when considering him as a [potential] companion. This does not diverge from—but supports my sentiment of the importance of compatibility in romance—the idea of being mated *and* matched.

While the observation of a potential mate's character is important, psychologist Dr. John K. Jacob voices his concern that personality is also something to take into account. He brings to light this disparity in male and female bonding which he calls the XY theory. *The XY Theory* is also the name of the book he authored in which he uses statistics to show that there is a twenty-five percent chance that we will choose

---

[7] Ellen G. White, *The Adventist Home*, 44.

a partner who can truly make us happy. He says that whether we are single or married, studies show that the problem in many romantic partnerships is personality incompatibility. Each person has an X or Y type personality; and when we are mismatched, problems will be inevitable.

I was fortunate enough to attend his seminar where I learned a great deal about myself by way of behavior patterns. This behavior patterning revealed my personality type and helps indicate who is a good romantic match for me. After attending his seminar and considering my relationship behavior patterns, I did research and found his theories to be something worth taking into consideration. Much of what the theory suggests is also consistent with my ideology of courtship and dating.

Dr. Jacob professes that each of us has a mask, or a natural facade, that we use in the dating scene. When what we sought after is attained, the mask fades away.

The XY Institute believes this facade is the social personality, which is different from our dating personality. The X personality type requires a lot of communication or intimacy. On the other hand, the Y personality type has a much lower need for communication or intimacy in a romantic relationship. How does this cause a problem? If a woman is an X, she may want to speak to her significant other for most of the day. She may also need regular words of affirmation and compliments. If her significant other is a Y type, he would not be interested in communicating that frequently throughout the day. At the beginning of the relationship, he may conform to her desire in order to appease her and win her affection. However, after a while, to him, her needs may seem to be problematic, and frankly annoying.

Could this be why your relationship is rocky? Does this theory explain why your relationship ended before it began, and would knowing it have saved you much time and grief?

Jacob's theory also challenges the well-known idea that opposites attract. He feels that though opposites may attract, he believes that they do not always stick. For more information and to take his personality test, visit his website at jacobresearchinstitute.net.

Another approach that takes personality and character into account is one by Pastor Alan Parker. In his presentation "Dating Isn't for Cowards," he said that each of us has a half-filled "love cup" that we all desire to be filled. Parker stresses that it is only Christ who can fill this cup. Nevertheless, we naturally desire people and things to fill our cup, and this makes way for idolatry. In other words, when you feel lonely and don't seek Christ to first fulfill this loneliness, you are seeking a relationship that can quite easily become idolized, making the potential partner your god. This is the perfect criterion for a potentially failed relationship. Pastor Parker strongly believes that when a relationship is based on infatuation or one person's happiness, it becomes a relationship based on manipulation. He states that courtship is or should be based on, and driven by, ministry. His interpretation of Ephesians chapter five is of a woman who will naturally love her husband. As the caregiver, the woman's desire to love is innate. Paul goes on to advise the woman to respect her husband and submit lovingly to him. He adds that the husband should love his wife because he may lose sight of this with the many distractions of the world. Parker reviews many different dating models but suggests one (from which he gets some inspiration) from the Bible and ideas from

Joshua Harris's book *I Kissed Dating Goodbye*. Parker stresses the importance of why he does not agree with dating. Some of those views are:

1. Dating leads to intimacy, but not necessarily commitment.
2. Dating confuses feelings for friendship.
3. Dating isolates persons from other meaningful platonic or familial relationships.
4. Dating distracts.
5. Dating causes discontentment with singleness.

Parker cautions against a traditional courtship approach that relies exclusively on group dating. In his opinion, group dating, though safer than isolated dating, doesn't allow you to learn as much information about the person you are considering. He believes a man and woman should first surrender their all to God, learn who they are in God, discover God's will for their lives, and then seek his will for their romantic life. Whether or not courtship is in God's will, you can still find contentment and satisfaction as a single person. When you become whole in Christ first, you do not need anyone else to complete you. Parker advises women to first become friends with the person whom they may be considering. You should also spend time in prayer and be prudent in observing a man's character.

1__1 = 1

Moreover, Parker suggests that problems arise in relationships because two individuals, who aren't compatible, use addition instead of multiplication. When God brought Adam and Eve together, it was multiplication—one times one, and they became one. When two very different people come together, it's math—one plus one, which equals two different people. Parker presents his model for dating. His first point is to become whole in Christ. Each individual should first discover who he or she is in the Lord first. He implores individuals considering courtship and marriage to develop a strong relationship with Jesus Christ and have Him harness his or her skills. God needs to cultivate you and help you to be temperate and have self-discipline. In God, as a young woman or young woman, you must develop your own personality. When you base your interest on togetherness, you allow someone else's persona to captivate you, and you become engulfed in that person and his lifestyle. This is how you lose your identity and opportunity to be happy in a relationship.

Your identity is in our Savior.

Self-Identity

She loved so hard,
she lost herself.
Even started to breathe like him.
That way she murdered herself in
who he was.
She no longer knew
who she was.

Don't love hard; love smart. Love is until death and then life everlasting. If love is ruining you and hindering your growth and character for eternal life, spend even more time in the Master's care. In the expression of love, there should be practicality; it's about being rational. Love doesn't compel you to lose yourself; it helps you find yourself. It encourages growth and isn't focused on only one individual. Have you buried your dreams for the sake of your partner's happiness? God calls two to come together in harmony to finish the work of His kingdom while retaining their individual identities in Him. Relationships are about two coming together, selflessly, to reap the very best versions of their individual selves.

[Ladies,] you are now to learn your first practical lessons in regard to the responsibilities of married life. Be sure to learn these lessons faithfully day by day... In your life union, your affections are to be tributary to each other's happiness. Each is to minister to the happiness of the other. This is the will of God concerning you. But while you are to blend as one, neither of you is to lose his or her individuality in the other. God is the owner of your individuality. Ask this of him: What is right? What is wrong? How may I best fulfill the purpose of my creation? "Ye are not your own; for ye are bought with a price: therefore glorify God in your body, and in your spirit, which are God's."[8]

Based on Parker's research, marriage doesn't make couples happy. In fact, research shows that people who are unhappy before marriage will continue to be unhappy after marriage. Happiness must exist within each person prior to marriage. He also warns against expressing interest too soon. This changes the nature and dynamics of a friendship.

Parker's second point is to do your homework! Observe the other person's character. Consider his God-given talents. Do this person's gifts complement yours? Can you two put your gifts together to produce a ministry and do the work of Christ as one? Parker also believes in knowledge before commitment. Know whom you are deciding to court. Inquire

---

[8] Ellen G. White, *Testimonies for the Church*, vol. 7.

about the individual. With his consent (so you don't seem too creepy), speak with a couple of his closest friends and family to develop an understanding of who he is. Ask as many questions as possible while praying. In regards to doing homework, some others have also suggested doing background checks before dating. I would say to do whatever makes you feel safe and confident without violating anyone's privacy or breaking the law.

Third, Parker highlights the importance of being patient. Spend much time in prayer seeking God's guidance on this critical area of your life. As, Ellen G. White stated, "Make haste, slowly, pure love will take God into all its plans."

Another helpful tool I extracted from Parker's seminar is this arrangement of priority:

1. Christ—make Christ the center, the reason, and the first priority.
2. Communication—consider communication skills. Is he a good listener? Is he a good conversationalist? Develop good communication skills with him.
3. Conflict resolution—consider his or her approach and ability to resolve conflicts. This will be vital to know before you consider this person as a mate. Is he or she active, passive, proactive or reactive? Are you active, or passive? Do you take the lead on conflict resolving approach, or do you sweep matters under the rug? Now, based on his style and yours, are you two compatible?
4. Commitment to ministry—is he a true Christian? Does he or she love the Lord? Has he or she accepted the call to ministry? Remember, being spiritual doesn't begin

and end at going to church. Just having the potential to be a Christian does not cut it.
5. Chemistry—is there attraction? Is there a natural connection between you two? Or does conversation and interaction feel forced?

Lastly, Parker makes these other suggestions: Consider his or her lifestyle, doctrinal beliefs, and personality. Seek prudent counsel from older and wiser spiritual persons. Never allow intimacy to get ahead of commitment, and don't allow commitment to come before knowledge. Consider the other person's money-spending habits and ability to manage a home.

Before compatibility is considered, each person should take note of him or herself. If you are ready for a romantic relationship, are you the right mate for whom you're seeking?

Dr. Kay Kuzma makes a couple of suggestions in her book, *Serious About Love*, about readying oneself for the right mate. According to her experiences, first, each individual must accept themselves. You should not be seeking companionship for happiness or security. If your partner isn't happy with whom they are first, this may cause an emotional dependency.

She claims:

If you need someone's presence in order to feel secure and comfortable, you are likely to try and control that person to keep him or her as close to you as possible. During the first few months after marriage, it might feel rewarding to meet the dependence needs of a mate. But it won't take long for this responsibility to become a burden from which the mate will want to escape. Relationships are a burden and not a blessing. Each individual should be dependent on

Christ to fulfill their individual role in the relationship, and sustain the bond of their union.[9]

How can you be sure that you won't marry another person because you need that person to feel fulfilled? Concentrate on valuing and accepting yourself. If you don't like who you are, the chances are great that you will try to find a partner who makes you feel better about yourself. When you use a person to meet your unmet needs, that's how emotional dependence begins.

You may even feel as if you cannot live without this person; however, this is the wrong sentiment to have for your significant other. If something were to happen to your partner, how would you deal with this situation?

Kuzma suggests the following to be a great mate:
1. Accept yourself.
2. Understand your value to God. Realize that nobody is perfect.
3. Take an honest look at yourself.
4. Evaluate your progress.
5. Deal with the pathology of your past.
6. Make mature decisions
7. Develop a spiritual life.

She then makes suggestions for growing good relationships:
1. Be friendly.
2. Be positive—smile inside and out.
3. Look attractive.
4. Be a good conversationalist.
5. Do and act your best wherever you are.

---

[9] Dr. Kay Kuzma, *Serious About Love,* (Pacific Press, 2009).

6. Go places where you'll meet the right kind of people.
7. Be interesting; do interesting things; go interesting places, etc.

Kuzma further expands on these suggestions in her book.

As it relates to compatibility, how often is the notion of commonality ignored? The unstableness of relationships can be attributed to several factors. These factors can be divided into different areas such as; religious, social, personal, economic, educational, and ethnic.[10]

Based on my extensive research, I've concluded that commonalities are often ignored or disregarded as it relates to male and female relationships. I've found that relationships tend to be more successful when couples share more than just common interests—hobbies, goals, likes/dislikes, and so on—but also similar ethnic backgrounds, the same religious orientation or denomination, are similar in age, educational background, health and eating practices and ideas of health consciousness, and familial background as it pertains to cultural values. This would include upbringing, the core family beliefs, and their parents' parenting styles. There are exceptions to these circumstances, of course. However, the more common ground to share, the higher the success rate.

---

[10] Dr. Alanzo H. Smith and Dr. June A. Smith, *Why Good Relationships Turn Bad: What To Do About It* (Columbus: Brentwood Christian Press, 2002), 123.

Unequally-Yoked

Can two walk together, except they be agreed?[11]

I have been shown the cases of some who profess to believe the truth, who have made a great mistake by marrying unbelievers. The hope was cherished by them that the unbelieving party would embrace the truth; but after his object is gained, he is further from the truth than before. And then begin the subtle workings, the continued efforts, of the enemy to draw away the believing one from the faith.

Many are now losing their interest and confidence in the truth because they have taken unbelief into close connection with themselves. They breathe the atmosphere of doubt, of questioning, of infidelity. They see and hear unbelief, and finally they cherish it. Some may have the courage to resist these influences, but in many cases their faith is imperceptibly undermined and finally destroyed.[12]

In 2 Corinthians 6:14, Paul states, "Be ye not unequally yoked together with unbelievers: for what fellowship hath righteousness with unrighteousness? and what communion hath light with darkness?"

When Paul wrote this, he was addressing believers of the God of the Bible, urging them to refrain from intermarrying with unbelievers—believers of other gods. We can even apply this warning to friendships. To analyze this warning on a deeper level, I would like to consider applying it to courting outside of your denomination. When God inspired these words through Paul, not that this was His desire, He knew that thousands of denominations would rise

---

[11] Amos 3:3
[12] White, *Letters*, 29.

up out of Christianity, having various beliefs and ideologies. A person's religious persuasions are not only limited to their belief in God. Your religious persuasions also influence and govern your style of dress, the music you may listen to, the food you eat, your ideas of marriage and courtship, the places you decide to go, and as a result, who you are as an individual. So, regardless of whether two people believe in the same God, their individual denominations may have different practices, doctrinal beliefs, interpretations on scripture, and cause the two to be different or incompatible.

If the two persons do not agree on the same health habits, as far as vegetarianism and meat-eating, or which meats are safe and clean to eat, or which day they will attend church, does this not cause conflict? If they become married and decide to have children, will they come to an agreement on how their children will be raised? These are all questions that I believe should be discussed in the very early stages of intentional friendship. Your beliefs may change, and the possibility of one converting to the other's religion is possible. However, I do not believe these preferences should be ignored and dealt with after the "I do!"

Culture and Religion

I have found similarities in ethnicity and culture to be important. However, there is a distinct culture found within religion and denomination also. Whenever this culture exists within religion there may be less concerns of incompatibility. For instance, as it relates to bi-racial dating, if two people are of the same religion or denomination, the practices of that denomination may draw more areas of commonalities, depending on whether or not the beliefs or doctrines of the particular denomination is practiced. Race has a big impact on us culturally and who we are as individuals; it may influence our choice of music, types of foods we eat, the things we deem important, and so on. These things are also impacted by religious persuasions.

Chapter 7
Help from God

God's Timing

Sometimes the only thing wrong is the timing. Observe it, make necessary actions, and respect it for what it is. He won't notice you too late. It is all in God's timing.

YOU DESERVE MORE

I wanna love you like I want to breathe.
But I would rather rest in peace than war with this inclination to hurt you.
I want to give you everything!
Unclothe the nakedness of my soul that
I've only ever shared with God. But no, not like this.
I need to have a heart whole
before I can love with my whole heart.
You deserve more than just these cold and distracted pieces of me.
The most beautiful piece
of broken art may want your affection when

you can't give it everything
it needs. So, instead of being selfish, time would rather give
you nothing than give you half
of what you deserve.

Timing Is Everything

When a man grabs a woman by the heart, it can be either one of the most beautiful things that has ever happened to her or one of the most dangerous things that will ever happen to her.

Many of us are not yet ready for courtship. As human beings, we often find ourselves in relationships with individuals who are right for us, but the timing may not be according to God's plan. And why is that? God's timing is perfect. He's always ready to give us what we need, but he's just waiting for us to be ready to receive it. For others, marriage may not even be in their will. Yet the biggest issue facing countless individuals is the erroneous notion that they need another person to complete them. Upon exiting a relationship, one is often left broken, distressed, hurt, and insecure. Nevertheless, jumping back into another relationship is not the solution. Pursuing a relationship when you are not ready to be in one, especially if it is with the wrong individual, will only continue to confuse you and fill you with resentment for the opposite sex. Pursue God. Allow Him to fix you. A relationship with God should be your foremost pursuit.

The Beauty in Single

One of the stupidest things I've ever done is also a lesson I will never forget. When I was about fifteen years old, I was at summer camp, and we went cliff jumping in New Hampshire. Now, I did not know how to swim, but for some strange reason I was not aware of this at that moment. I guess it was because of the excitement of everyone jumping from the cliff into the deep blue. The pressure of the onlookers around me, sizing me up with their critical stares, didn't help either. I can still hear them chanting, "Do it! Do it!" So without hesitation, I marched up to the edge of the cliff, braced myself, and leaped to my jump of doom. Again, I did not know how to swim at all! I plunged into the dark, cold water like a bowling ball, sinking without compromise. Thankfully, the man who was near me when I dropped noticed I had not resurfaced and dived in to save my life. This was quite a traumatizing experience and left me with a serious fear of deep waters.

A couple of years later, my family and I went on a cruise. The cruise ship let us board a smaller boat that stopped far off the coast of a beach in the Bahamas. Once again, I had to face my fear of water. Strapped into a life vest this time, I was still reluctant to venture into the shallows, making it very apparent as I tiptoed into the water. I was cautious in my approach and patient with myself as I remembered my experience.

A huge dilemma facing many is the erroneous notion that they need another person to complete them. After experiencing a bad breakup, you're often left broken, distressed, hurt, and insecure. Diving back into another relationship heart first is not the answer. Help us break the stigma that disqualifies you as a competent human living alone as a single. If you're not ready to be in a relationship, especially if it's with the wrong individual, you will only continue to allow yourself to be miserable, distraught, and confused. Break the cycle where you are never learning from your mistakes or learning about yourself as an individual.

So many men and women are drowning in discouragement, depression and desperation; so they grab on to the closest person they see thinking a relationship will save them. In my experience in the Bahamas, it would not have been wise for me to jump back into the deep water, especially after what I had experienced at my summer camp. I should've never jumped off a cliff into deep water when I did not know how to swim. What I learned was that I had to be ready before I engaged. Before you pursue a romantic commitment, you have to be emotionally and mentally healthy. This implies understanding your potential mate's emotional and physical needs, and it entails thorough knowledge of not only the individual whom you are interested in, but also of yourself. After a breakup and after you get to know yourself and learn from your past mistakes, are you ready to be in another relationship? Whether you are or not, resume with caution. Often, in these situations, we cannot trust ourselves. It's always best to seek counsel from older and wiser godly individuals.

I am not here to lie to you; a relationship may or may not be in God's will for you. Maybe you'll get married, maybe not. Regardless of how bitter or sweet the fruit of your love life is, singleness is a blessing. You're not unworthy of love. You're not a darkened sun—you are a golden cloud. You are a white ocean, a beautiful wave of woman, nothing of ugly. You are not detestable. We men long for you. We are still learning how to love you. Still bracing to swim the depth of your devotion. Still longing to wing your sky. So please do not continue to trail around this globe with ghostly hope. Do not trade off on life. God loves you more than the heart longs for the taste of blood. He is love and the epitome of it. He created your smile and knows how to work it. Follow Him wherever He goes. He will never mislead you.

There is nothing wrong with being single. I wish someone would've told me this years ago! It is not a disease. Yes, at times you will feel lonely, and you definitely want a fulfilling life. However, don't compromise your long-term happiness for the sake of being in a relationship. I think we place too much emphasis on the idea of being in a relationship to the point that we cannot live without being in one.

There is plenty of room for happiness in singleness. Spend some quality time with yourself, and show yourself why someone would want to be happy with you! You may be blocking your potential blessing. God may be withholding courtship from you because he knows you will idolize your relationship. Relationships are a wonderful thing, and it feels good to be loved. But the word *single* is synonymous with happiness too. And someone does love you. His name is Jesus.

NIGHTLY VISITORS

Every day I woke up asleep on his love.
Head resting on his dampened memories
I would hold these tears if only they
weren't so heavy.
His daring smile, persistent charm.
The way the cello in his voice sang.
I pull up these things to keep me safe from the
lonely frost creeping through the room.
Misery loves company,
this miserable gust of pain.
Darkest part about it was falling
asleep at night. At night, asleep,
I saw him. Lying next to me.
Piercing me. His heart was reopened.
Smile dug in his face.
In the corner of my room,
two pieces of luggage.
Looks like he was back to stay.
But when the sun's rays bled through
the blinds,
Left there dead,
I was bloody, accursed.
Rotting in these memories.

When all that remains of something you expected to last are memories, you'll have a hard time erasing them. Don't be too hard on yourself. Sometimes, it's best to consider your memories as a type of coping mechanism. I know you wish the thoughts were a seed you could plant, watching it grow and bloom back into the reality of the two of you. However, after a while, the memories too must die and be buried, never to be seen or heard of again.

Maybe this time good-bye was permanent, or maybe not. Regardless, refuse to put your life on hold. Continue to stay busy and channel your energy into learning from your mistakes to make yourself better for you first and maybe for when he returns. Moreover, if love finds you again for someone else, you will be in a better place for both yourself and the person you end up with.

God's Timing Is Perfect
(YOU ARE WORTH THE WAIT)

Her smile whispers.
I see in oblivion.
Her love for God comes in four-wheel drive.
This is what I race for.
We only explode each other's hearts a sunrise ago.
I do not mind waiting the rest of my moons
to grow into her orbit.
I'll be poems like this until she realizes
they spell her name.
They breathe her.
Only a fool will either heed
to the instigating of impatience or
allow it to mold him into believing he can
win an argument with time.
Snatching the pen out of God's hands
to write his fate.
Forging the signature of his
own destiny.

I know better, though.
I've waited my whole life wondering
if time ever existed.
To find out it does
but not with you.
We melt into the future.
Dripping under the sun, we
love like mischievous tide.
I won't rush our transformation.
I will wait for love.
After all these windy ideas of praying and hoping.
A couple of extra holidays won't hurt me.

These holidays where families rekindle.
I see you in every smile that breaks in front me.
Time is a game.
Has a good way of reminding you
of what you don't have while
hinting toward what you may.
Our time has a bad memory,
or selective, how these good moments are eternal.
We both win.
They say timing is everything.
I say God is everything, and patience is
one of his ways of reminding us of that.
Time is betting these stories I write
about you aren't fiction but friction.
To start a flame that will burn like a
summer rain. Drops
on AC, our
prelude tap dancing.

You hum to the sound, not even realizing
that everything you've never tasted
is growing under the music of the
raindrops.

Our great garden thoughts.
Fruit melody memories.
I know it seems like my mind is
moving too quickly, but
I am not rushing things.
I am anticipating the
inevitable.
Bracing destiny.
All times, ten out of ten,
eventually knowing gives in.
Time never does well when it comes
to keeping secrets.

Respect your time and the time of others too. If there is no future, there is no point. I would not suggest courtship if marriage is not your long-term goal. While you wait, I would also suggest valuing your body and guarding your heart. You need to know you are worth the wait.

You aren't just out to catch him in a lie. You want to trust him. You want to love him more than anything. You just want to know that you're important to him. He needs to be open and honest. He should voluntarily tell you who all his lady friends are. He should've told these friends about you. He needs to show you that he cares. He needs to show you that he's there and isn't going anywhere.

Finding the Right One

In order to meet the person you want to meet, first be the person you would want that person to meet. Focus your time and energy on discovering who you are. Find pleasure in who you are as a person, spending less time focusing on your loneliness and longing desire for courtship. Spend more time working on you. This is something I had to discover and go through as well!

It's You

It was
seven months into
our endearing scenery.
To feel us.
Feel the candescent bulb of your stomach.
Our collage of endless.
We laughed like an estranged tomorrow.
Smiling like a valley.
Making swing of our hands.
Orchestra grass of lilies airborne
spring up in song.
Park bench in boisterous stance.
Modeling his new wood.
Ushering us in for a seat.
We did.
Contracting in his grace.
There at that moment,
I was born in your eyes.
I remember your clingy appetite.
You staring like fragile water.
Also remember when you first called me baby.

These are my lagging memories.
Born in my mind and stuck still.
Our stillborn
love.
Dwindled hope.
When we celebrated our first spring,
I wanted to crawl into the summers with you.
Our first steps into the moonlight.
God catching us if we ever fall.
Determined to warm the winter with you.
This is what remains.
These thoughts
provoking.
Where everything is a prideful perfect.
My brave heart still moping around.
This leaky pen
on these tired lines.
The only thing that left
is
you.

We had the Milky Way in common.
But this one thing.
Never seen eye to eye.
That's 'cause I
never left.
But you never
stayed.
Been a couple of months now.
Somehow got lazy with my emotions.
Ended up right back in that park.

Bench still here
but mocking me with his
splintered eyes.
I splintered. Why
couldn't I unlearn being a fool for you?
Doctor scolding me saying
what's left of us is dead
you and your reproach saying
we never were alive.
After nine months,
"love" didn't really ring.
You said it was too premature for that name.
Why? I've waited a jaded
twenty-something years to show you.
Hold you.
Introduce my lungs to the newborn of your smell.
Worked so hard to stare into your happy.
All I got was a lukewarm smile.
Guess that's why labor pains.

You said late is a cliché excuse for never.
You're comfortable not being here as if
you never were.
As if you never were invited.
I tried to give us an invitation to live.
Why would it be in His will for us to perish?
I gave the night sky insomnia how carefully I prayed for you.
Time can probably rinse out these feelings.
Not even death can bleach out this love.
Left here.
The most patient wedding party.

My lonely tuxedo.
The staccato flavor of your kiss...
Yes this, our wedding,
stained with stubborn love
and somber hope,
still lives.
Only thing that died
is
you.

Christ is the giver and sustainer of life. Right now, you too are afraid to love while Christ is knocking at the door of your heart. The enemy of your soul wants to pen your story. He wants nothing more than for you to ignore His entreaties so that you will be left without a savior and die.

A Happy Ending

Your story can have a happy ending. The single woman in her late thirties is always painted to be dark and unsightly. She may even take on the persona of this accepted view and think herself to be accursed. I refute this idea. You are beautiful and significant as a single or married individual. Men too suffer from this misdiagnosis.

In most cultures, a man is usually only successful after accomplishing three things: gaining some type of wealth, purchasing his own home, and marriage/a family. Success is subjective. Furthermore, a man's success is not a main determinant of his marital status. I do believe that romantic relationships are a beautiful blessing from God. Although many may have the wrong idea of romantic relationships and misguided views of marriage, I do believe that distressing and unsuccessful marriages are avoidable.

Husbands may taste heaven in their wives. Wives may taste heaven in their husbands. And the world may taste heaven in your marriage. To be hope, a blessing, a reliever of distress, sadness, and grief, to be like Jesus is the high calling and standard God has for His people.

GRACE

You should let him love you. He won't be perfect.
But, may promise to be good at it.
Like every night after thanking God for the day He decided
he was man enough to know your name.
And every night, he will praise Him like He's forgetful.
For the way your skin is the sunrise.
The sunrise of a Sunday sun, after the Son rose.
The sun, roses,
and you, and him decorating your favorite seashore.
See? He's sure about
forever. This is to say, he's decided on eternity.
He will love you like Christ loves
His church. In His heart beats your future.
In His will, there's a you and him.

As beautiful as marriage is, it takes a lot of dedication and work! God does not simply allow two individuals to meet. He entrusts the two to vow, bearing a revelation of the sacred principle of love before this dying world and the spotless worlds while accepting Christ into their hearts as a Helper. If God blesses you with someone to love, understand He is holding you accountable and responsible for how you treat the wonderful gift of love and the beautiful person's soul He died for.

I brought to light several topics which I consider pertinent, some based on real stories and/or experiences. I have also done much research. After reading this book, you may continue to date and reject courtship altogether. I think you deserve more. Courtship will not be perfect, but it surely is better. Courtship, like dating, will have hard times; you may argue and fight but through prayer and faith in God, you will fight together.

Romantic relationships push the innermost self to the surface. In a relationship, you clearly begin to see your selfishness or defensiveness and a host of other character deficiencies. After seeing yourself for who you are, you can choose to surrender to the perfect and wonderful Son of God. By having faith in Him, you are able to overcome your flaws.

You may or may not agree with my viewpoints and the viewpoints of others made in this book (and do not have to), but I hope you do take them into consideration. I deem the issues surrounding the dating scene to be serious, yet underemphasized. It is my wish that this book has brought information, inspiration, insight, and empowerment as well as help and hope to those countless women and men who are hurting or have been hurt. That it will bring restoration to many. God bless you!

Thank You

Thank you for embarking on this journey with me. It has been a long one, but I hope it was fruitful. I've dedicated my time to uplifting you in prayer. I pray for the individuals who will read this book. So wherever you are, whatever your circumstances may be, regarding love, and romance, dating or courtship, I am praying for you. I pray we are all ready for the eminent and very soon return of our Lord and Savior, Jesus Christ. May God bless you and keep you.

More from the Author

If you appreciated this book, you will want to read more from Sean.

The Most Beautiful Arrangement of Broken

By Sean L. Brereton

A woman, at first appearing as damaged and cowed by a failed relationship, is gradually transformed by her meeting with a man who sees her worth and helps her on a spiritual road to finding depth and meaning in a true bond. In this collection of poetry, *The Most Beautiful Arrangement of Broken*, written by Sean L. Brereton, the reader is taken on a journey of immense beauty and grace, set amongst a wheel of verses which tell of a delicate tale of passion, rejection, and ultimately, love. There really is something for all of us in these poems, and the use of language which is sometimes contemporary but also evokes the sentiment of another era, will leave the reader with an unquenchable thirst for more.

The Redefinition of a Man

By Sean L. Brereton

Manhood is not determined by age, but by the decision to be responsible, to love and respect yourself and others. Brooklyn native, Sean L. Brereton, took some time to arrive at this fact. Growing up, his particular view of women and definition of what it means to be a man was influenced by his once-cherished music and the culture he was most attracted to. It wasn't until he realized that his perception of masculinity and love had been tainted, that he was able to see the error of his ways. Despite what society seems to perpetuate, Brereton's view of manhood is now very different.

In *Redefinition of a Man*, he delivers an intense and profound work, drawing on the experiences of his past, facts of his present, and the dreams of a bright future. His view of true manliness centers on putting God first and everything else second, giving his work a deep and powerful sincerity. Brereton's unique voice gives this collection strength and power. Immerse yourself, become inspired, and be encouraged with *Redefinition of a Man*.

A Foretaste of Heaven

By Sean L. Brereton

More than ever, the pursuit of love becomes lost in the desert of desire and passion. Disappointment, hurt, and regret are usually common feelings afterwards. Is there a remedy? How can we avoid such heart-breaking situations? What can we do differently that will help us find the true love we seek, and build solid relationships that last?

In *A Foretaste of Heaven*, Brereton answers these questions and offers readers hope. His wisdom, practical advice, and insight prescribe the antidote for anyone seeking but failing to find true love. Through his own story, Brereton provides proof and explains how the path to happiness intersects with the word of God. God's Word offers you guidance and hope, as long as you are willing to seek it out and accept it. When one roots their relationship in Christ, they create a strong and lasting covenant of love, commitment, and faith. Return to God's plan and reap the rewards of what a true and honest courtship can bring to your life.

How to Order

1. Author's website—www.seanlbrereton.com
2. Amazon.com
3. BarnesandNoble.com

CONTACT ME

Please keep in touch by following me on Instagram:

@seanlbrereton

@whateverywomanneedstoknow

Follow me on Facebook:

www.facebook.com/aseyeseetheworld

Bibliography

1. Proverbs 3:5-6
2. Sean L. Brereton, The Most Beautiful Arrangement of Broken, i.
3. Sean L. Brereton, *The Most Beautiful Arrangement of Broken,* (Brooklyn, NY: Sean L. Brereton Books, 2015) 42.
4. Sean L. Brereton, *As the World Sees Me,* 46.
5. Matthew 11:28
6. Romans 12:2
7. Ellen G. White, *Messages to Young People* (Nashville, TN: Southern Publishing Association, 1930), 31,32.
8. John 14:6
9. Ellen G. White, *Letters to Young Lovers* (Mountain View, CA: Pacific Press Publishing Association, 1983), 74.
10. Sean L. Brereton, As the World Sees Me, 74.
11. Ellen G. White, *The Adventist Home* (Hagerstown, MD: Review and Herald Publishing Association, 1952), 44.
12. Ellen G. White, *Testimonies for the Church,* vol. 7 (Mountain View, CA: Pacific Press, 1948)
13. Dr. Alanzo H. Smith, Dr. June A. Smith, Why Good Relationships Turn Bad What To Do About It.
14. Amos 3:3
15. Ellen G. White, Letters to Young Lovers, 29.

Made in the USA
Middletown, DE
14 April 2017